I0202408

When Grace Whispers

A Journey from Pain to Purpose

Sarah Osinowo

"When Grace Whispers: A Journey from Pain to Purpose"
Copyright: © 2025 Sarah Osinowo. All rights reserved
Phone: +44 7947 799 447
Email: funmib.osinowo@hotmail.co.uk

ISBN: 978-1-911312-37-6

Published by: Lacepoint
www.lacepointpublishing.com
books@lacepointpublishing.com

No part of this book may be reproduced, stored in a
retrieval system, or transmitted by any means without
the written permission of the author.

Scripture taken from the New King James Version®.
Copyright © 1982 by Thomas Nelson. Used by
permission. All rights reserved.

Any persons depicted or mentioned in this book are
purely fictional and is not subject to comparison with
any person, living or dead.

Cover design by Lacepoint

Printed in The Republic of Ireland.

Dedication

To the God who turns pain into purpose and
scars into testimonies.
And to every survivor who has ever felt unseen,
unheard, or broken—you are not alone.

Acknowledgement

First and foremost, I give all glory and thanks to God, who has been my all in all through this temporary journey of life on earth. Without His grace and guidance, this book would never have come to fruition.

To my husband Bamidele and our gifts Oluseun, Oluwafemi, and Oluwalayomi. Thank you for your unwavering love, support, and prayers. Your encouragement gave me the strength to start, continue and finish this book.

To the protagonist, special thanks. I am grateful to God for the strength He gave you to share your pain for the encouragement of many.

A heartfelt thank you to Lacepoint publishers and team who helped shape these words with wisdom and care. Your belief in this book means more than words can express.

4

Finally, to every reader, whether you are a survivor or have been blessed not to have experienced being silenced, ashamed or broken or not, thank you for embarking on this journey. May this book remind you that healing is possible and that God's love restores all things.

Contents

Disclaimer

The narrative presented in this book is inspired by real-life events; however, it is a work of fiction. While the locations mentioned in the story are real, they do not represent the actual places where the events occurred. All names have also been deliberately altered, and any resemblance to real individuals, whether living or deceased, is purely coincidental and unintentional.

Foreword

This book "When Grace Whispers: A Journey from Pain to Purpose" is inspired by a true story. However, due to the sensitive nature of the subject matter, the author has taken great care to protect the identity of the protagonist. While certain elements have been woven into the narrative for depth and engagement, the pain and suffering endured by the main character remain authentic. The core message of the story has been preserved to ensure that its impact is not diminished, allowing readers to connect with the grief, trials, and endurance of the protagonist.

The author has also sought to accurately portray the cultural context of the time in which the events unfold, even though the exact locations have been modified.

Physical, emotional and sexual abuse within family settings are harsh realities that many choose to ignore, often out of fear, shame, or cultural taboos. However, to live in denial of these issues is to deceive oneself and remain blind to the suffering of countless victims.

Silence and avoidance only enable perpetrators, allowing the cycle of abuse to persist across generations. Acknowledging this painful truth is the first step toward protection, healing, and justice. Ignorance may feel comfortable, but it comes at the cost of those who suffer in silence.

Through the pages of this book, you will witness not only the depths of human suffering but also the power of resilience, faith and grace of God.

Above all, the purpose of this book is to offer hope to those who may have faced similar hardships. For the reader to know that they are not alone, as we are admonished in 1 Corinthians 10:13 (NKJV).

"No temptation has overtaken you except such as is common to man; but God is faithful, who will not allow you to be tempted beyond what you are able, but with the temptation will also make the way of escape, that you may be able to bear it."

If you see yourself in these pages, do not despair. Reach out for help. Turn to the Almighty God, our Heavenly Father, for He alone can truly heal the brokenhearted and bind up their wounds (Psalm 147:3). He will remove the burden of resentment and set you free to live a new life, unshackled from the failures of others. And even more importantly, break the cycle of abuse from continuing across generations.

Just as God rewrote Ella's story, He can rewrite yours—not merely as that of a survivor, but as one who has triumphed. Through the whisper of

11

His grace, He will redeem, restore, and rebuild your life by His love and redemption that can transform even the darkest past into a testimony of victory and make all things new for you. (Revelation 21:5)

Isekhua Evborokhai

Author of Still Standing

Dundalk, Ireland

Prologue

ELLA SITS ON THE bench in the Dundalk Courthouse and observes all of the goings on. She wasn't there for any serious case but had been summoned to court for not holding a TV license, and was determined to plead not guilty due to extenuating circumstances.

She has been floating in and out of deep contemplation ever since she arrived. Her mind, like an open door, has become a battleground where relentless thoughts invade without invitation. They come swiftly, unannounced, seizing control of her peace before she has the chance to resist. These are not just ordinary thoughts — they are whispers from the shadows, sent by an unseen enemy determined to rob her of joy. Each one digs into the wounds she so desperately longs to heal, resurfacing pain she had prayed to leave behind. No matter how hard she tries to push them away, they persist, weaving themselves into the fabric of her mind, threatening to pull her back into a past she has fought so hard to escape.

A sudden gust of cold wind swept across her face, as someone came in through the automatic doors, sharp and unexpected, it cut through the fog of her wandering thoughts, sending a shiver down her spine, jolting her back to the present as if waking from a dream and back into the courthouse.

As she sat, waiting to be called she sees different people coming and going; some accused like her, others, staff of the court, etc. lawyers walking past in full regalia and all sorts of government officials.

Her court hearing was 10:30am but she had arrived at 9:50am and was told by a gentleman at the information desk that her case would be heard in courtroom 1, that he would call her when it was her turn and asked her to sit across in the waiting area.

The first case was called a few minutes later. Ella sees a female lawyer walk across the waiting lobby to another lady. A few minutes later the two of them returned with a third lady holding a folder on the side and Ella could make out the title, KJ vs BJ.

SB vs SB was the next case that was called. The man announcing the court cases appeared to take great pride in his role, confidently striding back and forth with a sense of self-assurance.

As she observes, she realizes that the courthouse was a different world altogether. What would her world have been like if life had presented her with different circumstances, she wondered.

Ella's childhood was marked by hardship. She faced abuse in many forms — physical, emotional, and sexual — and was constantly moved from place to place. Tragically, she never had the chance to truly know her mother, who passed away before Ella turned four.

Ella has always struggled to grasp even the faintest memory of her mother. Having lost her at such a young age, the details have long since slipped through her fingers like sand. She can't recall her mother's smile, the warmth of her touch, or the soothing hum of a lullaby — off-key or not. No matter how hard she tries, all that remains are fleeting impressions, fragments too blurred to piece together. Time and grief have stolen what little she might have held onto, leaving only an aching void where memories should be.

Ella's father, Henry, had moved to the States to pursue his studies, and it was there he met Suzanne, Ella's mother, who came from a wealthy family at the time. The details of how they met were never fully shared, but it was clear they were deeply in love, as they soon married. Not long after, Ella was born, followed by her younger brother, Noah, just 18 months later.

Eventually, Ella's case was called, alongside a few others who had been summoned for not having a TV license. One by one, she watched as the judge either dismissed the case or imposed a fine for the unpaid amount.

To Ella's surprise, her case was an anti-climax. She wasn't called to speak. Her name was read out, and because she had already purchased a license and had no prior offenses, her case was also struck off.

Relieved, she walked out of the courthouse and onto the quiet streets of Dundalk, her mind still filled with that lingering, persistent thought.

CHAPTER

1

Tragedy

"For the Lord will not cast off forever. 32 Though He causes grief, Yet He will show compassion According to the multitude of His mercies. 33 For He does not afflict willingly, Nor grieve the children of men."

Lamentations 3:31-33 (NKJV)

ELLA'S MOTHER TRAGICALLY passed away in 1969. Later, Ella was told that her mother had taken her own life. Despite her efforts to understand what led to this heartbreaking decision, she has never been able to uncover the full truth.

Various explanations have been offered. One suggestion was that her mother, frail and vulnerable, may have been taken advantage of by her husband, Henry. Another theory was that Henry had done something so shameful that her mother felt too embarrassed to face anyone.

Whatever the reason, it seemed that her mother felt the only way out was to end her life by drowning in the bathtub, with her two young children, Ella and Noah, sitting beside her.

Ella's aunt, Maria and her uncle, Steve had on different occasions described the heart-wrenching scene when the neighbours had heard the cries of Ella and Noah and, alarmed, called the police. The authorities arrived and broke down the doors, finding the children on the bathroom floor. Ella's mother was in the bath, having drowned. Her uncle revealed that, at the time of her death, her mother was to be buried as if she had no family. Henry had been arrested for an unrelated matter and was in custody, and there was no known contact with her mother's side of the family.

As a result, Ella and Noah were placed into foster care. Her uncle had to act quickly to prevent their mother from being buried as a nameless woman, and he reached out to the high commission for help. Thankfully, he was able to stop the burial until a family member could take charge. At that point, her grandfather, who was an acquaintance of the agent general for Nigeria, got involved. He went to the local authorities in New York and managed to find out where Ella and Noah were. The authorities confirmed that they had been placed in a foster home. With his intervention, Ella and Noah were taken out of the system, and they soon found themselves on a plane to Nigeria with an aunt, Mrs. Arnold, who was already traveling there.

Years later, Ella had reached out to her uncle, who had been close to both her parents during their time together. Her uncle shared what little he knew about her parents' lives, though much of it was clouded in mystery. He explained that her mother and father had moved around a lot, and he couldn't pinpoint exactly when they had met. What he did know was that he had become close to Henry, Ella's father, but the same couldn't be said for the rest of their family. By the time her mother passed away, they had become estranged from her side of the family, and no one seemed to know where they were living.

Ella's uncle told her that the first he knew about her mother's death came from an unexpected encounter with a mutual friend of Henry's who shared the devastating news with him.

Ella and Noah were so young at the time that they didn't even remember their mother. And even when they asked about her, relatives refused to share anything about her — their memories of her, her personality, her likes and dislikes. They were essentially erased from the family narrative. When they arrived in Nigeria, they were placed with their mother's relatives, and that's when the real challenges began.

CHAPTER

2

Abandoned

"Can a woman forget her nursing child,
And not have compassion on the son of
her womb? Surely they may forget, Yet I
will not forget you."
Isaiah 49:15 (NKJV)

ELLA HAD NEVER FELT more abandoned. That feeling had followed her like a shadow, lurking in the corners of her childhood, whispering that she was alone. From her earliest memories, she sensed that something was missing—a presence, a warmth, a love that should have been there but never was. The absence of her mother, the one person who should have offered her comfort and protection, was the most obvious void. Yet, it was more than that. It was the aching loneliness of never having anyone truly claim her, of never belonging anywhere.

Her childhood was spent moving from place to place, passed between relatives like an unwanted burden. From Benin to Agbor, and then to Lagos, where her mother's family had its roots, she never stayed long enough to put down roots of her own. At one point, she lived with her grandfather and his many children—some even younger than she was — but despite the house being full, it never felt like home. The constant uprooting prevented her from forming real connections. She was always the outsider, the extra mouth to feed, the child without a place.

Ella and her brother, Noah, were separated when they were still very young. She was sent to live with her mother's cousin, her cousin's husband, and their children. Her first clear memories were of starting primary school in that household. She vaguely recalled brief stays with her grandfather, but the details were blurry, like a distant dream she could never quite piece together. Before she could settle, she was moved again — this time to live with her maternal uncle.

Any hope of stability vanished when she realized what awaited her in her uncle's house. It wasn't a home; it was a place where she was tolerated at best, exploited at worst. Instead of being treated as a child in need of care, she became a servant. Babysitting, cooking, cleaning — these were her new responsibilities. Her aunt ruled the household with an iron grip, and Ella quickly learned that her role was to obey, to stay quiet, and to endure. She couldn't even remember if she attended school during this period; the days blurred into an endless cycle of chores and exhaustion. Her uncle, the one person who could have intervened, stood by in silence, either unwilling or unable to challenge his wife.

At night, when the house was finally quiet, Ella lay awake, haunted by the unanswered questions that tormented her. Why had her mother chosen to take her own life? What had been so unbearable that she had left Ella and Noah behind? And where was Noah now? Was he safe? Was he happy? Did he even remember her? These thoughts wrapped around her like chains, pulling her deeper into despair.

More than anything, she felt as though she was being punished — not for something she had done, but for simply existing. No matter how hard she worked, no matter how obedient she was, it was never enough. The mistreatment, the neglect, the feeling of being unwanted — it all became normal. She stopped expecting kindness. She stopped hoping for love. She withdrew into herself, her silence becoming her shield.

School should have been an escape, but instead, it was another reminder of how different her life was. Parent-teacher meetings, school performances, and special events were painful to sit through. While other children had parents cheering them on, Ella had no one. No uncle or aunt ever showed up for her, and sometimes, she wondered why she was even allowed to attend school at all.

At the age of eight, she was moved yet again—this time to live with her mother's immediate brother. It seemed like a fresh start, a chance to finally be with someone who might understand her pain. Her uncle, being her mother's brother, felt like the closest connection she had left to the mother she barely remembered. For a brief moment, she dared to hope that this time, things would be different. But hope had never been kind to Ella.

Her uncle's wife despised her from the moment she arrived. To her aunt, Ella was nothing more than an inconvenience, an unwanted responsibility. The hostility was immediate and relentless. Though her uncle tried to offer some protection, his efforts were futile. His wife dominated the household, her temper sharp and unpredictable. If she could turn her violence on her own husband—beating him so severely that he ended up in the hospital—what hope did Ella have of being treated with kindness?

The answer became clear soon enough. Ella had none. She was once again reduced to a servant. Her uncle and aunt had three young daughters, and Ella became their primary caregiver. Not only did she look after them throughout the day, but at night, she was expected to wake up to feed and change them. Her exhaustion was constant. She barely had time to breathe, let alone think about her own needs.

Her aunt worked as a teacher at the very school Ella attended, but that did not grant her any relief. Instead, it added another layer to her suffering. There was no break from the scrutiny, no space where she could relax. The exhaustion from her responsibilities at home made school almost impossible. By the time she arrived in the classroom, she was drained, her mind sluggish, her body aching. Concentration was a luxury she could not afford.

Her childhood was slipping away, swallowed by responsibility and silent suffering. Each time she was moved to a new home, she hoped it would be different. Each time, she was disappointed. She had been passed from one household to another, never truly belonging, never being loved, never being wanted.

More than anything, she longed for stability, for a place where she could simply be a child. But love and care remained out of reach, always a step away, always just beyond her grasp. The weight of hopelessness settled deep within her, growing heavier with each passing year, pressing down on her spirit, shaping the person she would become.

Ella had learned one truth early in life: she was alone, and she always would be. But she was wrong! Beyond the veil of her understanding, an unseen presence watched over her. The Unseen

Creator, the Maker of Heaven and Earth, had never taken His eyes off her — not for a single moment. His love had been woven into the very fabric of her existence, guiding her steps even when she felt lost. Though she could not yet see it, she was never truly alone.

CHAPTER

3

Darkness Falls

"Yea, though I walk through the valley of the shadow of death, I will fear no evil; For You are with me; Your rod and Your staff, they comfort me."

Psalm 23:4 (NKJV)

THE MOMENT ELLA stepped out of the courthouse, the sky darkened, and the rain resumed its steady downpour. Fat, warm droplets splattered against the pavement, carrying with them the familiar scent of wet earth and concrete. Without hesitation, she darted toward the nearest taxi, slipping into the back seat just as the rain intensified.

As she settled in, fastening her seatbelt, a memory surfaced—something she had overheard on the phone years ago while working in a call centre. The moment she mentioned that she was taking the call from Dublin, the South African on the other end chuckled and remarked that he had once heard an amusing description of Irish summers: "That's when the rain is warm." His comment playfully reflected the common perception of Ireland's famously unpredictable and often rainy weather. Implying that Ireland experiences constant rainfall throughout the year, with the only real distinction being the temperature of the rain — either cold in the winter or slightly warmer in the summer.

She had smiled at the thought then, and now, as the raindrops streaked the taxi window, she found herself musing over it again.

It had been a few good years since she made Dundalk her home. Here, she had finally found a sense of stability, a feeling that had once seemed elusive. It was somewhat similar to a couple of years ago when she lived with her uncle. Although it was a period she remembered as one of relative stability, where she had lived the longest, it however, wasn't perfect.

Ella's life had been filled with uncertainty and hardship, but when her uncle told her that her long-absent father, Henry, had returned from the United States and wanted to reunite with her and her brother, Noah, she was filled with a mix of hope and anxiety. Ella had never met her father, and the thought of finally living with him felt overwhelming. She had no idea what to expect, having spent the first eleven years of her life without any contact from him. The idea of reconnecting with Noah, who she hadn't seen in years, added to her unease.

Ella was living with her uncle and his family in Benin at the time, and her life had a steady rhythm there. But when her uncle arranged for her to move to Henry's house, everything changed. Her father's home was in a different part of the city, and Ella soon discovered that she was not only moving in with him but also with her stepmother, Janet, and her half-sister, Becky. This was a reality she had never prepared for, and despite her hopes for a fresh start, she had no idea of the painful reality that awaited her.

At first, things seemed promising. Ella was reunited with Noah, and for a brief moment, it seemed like they might finally have the family they had longed for. But as time passed, the facade of a happy family began to crumble. Her stepmother, harbouring a deep resentment for their presence, made life unbearable. Initially, the household chores were manageable — cooking and cleaning before school — but soon they turned into an all-consuming responsibility. Ella and Noah were punished for the smallest mistakes, often without explanation, and no matter how hard Ella tried, it was never enough for her stepmother.

The beatings became a daily occurrence. Her stepmother, Janet, would punish them for trivial reasons, such as not cleaning properly or making eye contact the wrong way. Ella felt as if she were constantly walking on eggshells, never knowing when the next punishment would come. She often shielded Noah from the worst of it, taking the blame for things he had done to protect him. The physical and emotional toll of living in such an environment became crushing. At times, Ella would escape to her uncle's house, seeking refuge from the abuse. But when her father found out, he forbade them from contacting their mother's side of the family, further isolating Ella and Noah.

The situation reached its breaking point after a particularly brutal beating, when Ella fled into the rain, seeking solace at her uncle's house once again. When she returned home, her father and stepmother promised not to harm her, but their promises were empty. As soon as her uncle and aunt left, the cruelty resumed, confirming to Ella that nothing would change. In that moment, all Ella could do was pray that she and Noah would survive, praying they wouldn't be maimed or killed by the very people who were supposed to care for them.

After a couple of years of torment, Ella's father's job took the family to Warri. The change of scenery did little to improve the situation at home. They lived on a well-maintained estate, Shell Camp, where Ella made friends, some of whom she still kept in touch with. But despite the new location, the damage had already been done. Ella had attended so many schools that she felt disconnected from her peers. At her new school, she was surrounded by children who had the stability she could only dream of. Her stepsister attended a private school on the estate, which only highlighted the differences in their lives. While Ella enjoyed a temporary escape when she was sent to school, she was still burdened with looking after her stepsister when she was sick. She became the family's designated childminder, a role she never wanted.

When Ella finished primary school and began her secondary education, her heart was no longer in it. The constant moving, the neglect, and the emotional abuse had drained her. Her time in school was marked by a deep sense of alienation and disconnection. The emotional toll of her home life left her unable to focus on her education, and she eventually had to retake some exams. During that time, she was once again relegated to endless chores. Her days were consumed with cooking, cleaning, and looking after her stepsister, leaving no time for rest or personal growth.

Despite the ongoing neglect and abuse, Ella found solace in school. It became her only escape, the only place where she could briefly forget the painful realities of her home life. But even at school, she was emotionally checked out. She would attend classes but often skip out halfway through, spending time with her friends to regain some sense of independence. This small act of rebellion, leaving school early, was one of the few ways Ella could regain some semblance of control in her chaotic life.

When Henry decided to start his own business and moved the family again, this time to Agbor, Ella hoped for a fresh start. But nothing changed. The dynamics at home remained the same. Her stepsister was treated like a princess, while Ella and Noah continued to be the outcasts. Despite everything, Ella endured, holding onto the hope that one day, she and her brother might escape the torment they were living through. Her journey, marked by constant upheaval, abuse, and neglect, showed Ella the strength it took to survive in a world that often felt cruel and unforgiving.

CHAPTER

4

The Wolf

"It would be better for him if a millstone were hung around his neck, and he were thrown into the sea, than that he should offend one of these little ones."

Luke 17:2 (NKJV)

ELLA COULD NOT REMEMBER exactly when the abuse started. One moment, she had been an innocent child, going about her days like any other, and the next, she was forced into a reality that was dark, disgusting, and beyond her understanding. It wasn't just the cruelty of her stepmother that tormented her — it was something far worse.

Henry, the man who was supposed to be her father and protector, had suddenly decided that he "loved" her in a way no father should. This was the same man she had once turned to, hoping he would see the suffering she endured under his wife's hand. Instead of protecting her, he became her worst nightmare. His idea of love was twisted and vile. Had he always been this way, or had something within him twisted over time, broken maybe?

Although he bore the physical likeness of her father, beyond that, he was nothing like the man she had once knew. Somewhere along the way, he had shed whatever goodness he might have had, if he did have any, revealing his true nature. Now, there was no doubt: he was a wolf in sheep's clothing, a dangerous predator lurking under the cover of a "loving father."

He would take Ella out in his car and force her to do things that made no sense to her young mind. Even as she grew older, she could never fully grasp the horror of what he had done to her.

Fear kept her silent. He made it clear that if she ever spoke of what was happening, he would kill her. And even if she did tell, he assured her, no one would believe her anyway. She was trapped. The abuse continued for years, stealing away any sense of normalcy she might have had.

When Ella finally made it to university, she thought she had escaped. But freedom came at a price. Her dad, who still held financial control over her, made sure she paid for every bit of independence she tried to claim. When she asked for money for school fees and upkeep, he would rather spend it on his girlfriend, leaving Ella to fend for herself. On the rare occasions when he did give her money, it was barely enough to get her back to campus, let alone survive.

Ella quickly realized that the only way to stay safe was to avoid going home altogether. During shorter holidays like Christmas and Easter, she stayed on campus, going hungry for days rather than risk returning. Sometimes, she stayed with friends — kind souls who welcomed her into their homes, unaware of the depths of her suffering. She would always be grateful to them; they had unknowingly saved her from a fate worse than death.

Summer holidays, however, were unavoidable as she had to return home. Lasting eight to ten weeks, they dragged her back into the nightmare that she could never fully escape from. The abuse would resume, and any attempt to resist or speak out was met with terrifying threats. Once, in desperation, she confided in her stepmother, hoping that, despite her cruelty, she would step in to protect her. It was a mistake.

Her stepmother, Janet, pretended to care, telling Ella to write down everything that had happened so she could confront Henry with it as evidence. And for the first time, Ella felt hope. She believed, naively, that she would finally be free of this monster. But instead of helping, her stepmother used the letter as blackmail, holding it over Henry to benefit herself and her daughter. Ella had thought she was turning to a mother figure for protection, but in reality, she had only handed over another weapon for her tormentor to use against her.

Her stepmother never once tried to help her, never once acknowledged her pain or offered her a way out. Instead, she chose to protect herself, ignoring the broken girl who had placed all her trust in her.

As soon as Ella's father realized that she had confided in Janet about his abuse, his anger boiled over, and he taunted her with cruel words. Sneering and questioning whether she truly believed that Janet could rescue her. He mocked and assured her that he knew Janet wouldn't help her, and that no one would come to her aid.

This betrayal shattered Ella in a way nothing else had. From that moment on, she stopped believing in the idea that anyone could save her. The world had proven time and again that she was utterly alone.

Ella sank deeper into despair. She became withdrawn, depressed, and suicidal. Every day, she asked herself when the suffering would end, when God would finally take her away from this life so she could feel normal again. University became a blur. She moved through her days like a ghost, barely holding on, surviving on whatever little she could find.

Unlike her peers, she dreaded going home. It was not a place of rest or reunion — it was a place of torment. She avoided it as much as she could, but the weight of it followed her everywhere.

Thankfully, the abuse did not persist during Ella's university days. She found ways to protect herself by strategically avoiding being alone with her father. During the holidays for instance, she sought refuge in the homes of close friends and their families. Additionally, she spent significant time with her maternal grandfather, creating distance between herself and the harmful environment at home.

Even on occasions when she had no choice but to return home for the holidays, she remained vigilant. Ensuring she was never left alone in the house with her father, and always found ways to keep herself surrounded by others.

In 1988, Ella graduated and, like every Nigerian graduate, was required to complete the National Youth Service Corps (NYSC). She was posted to Rivers State, and for the first time in her life, she experienced something close to freedom. Being away from home for an entire year was a gift, a chance to breathe without fear. She clung to the hope that she would be offered a permanent position at her workplace, that maybe, just maybe, she would never have to see her dad again. But life was never that kind to her.

The service ended after a year, and she had no choice but to return home. Some might have said that, as an adult, she could now stand up for herself. But the scars of childhood ran deep. In Nigeria, parents ruled their children with intimidation, and even in adulthood, the fear remained. Her dad had crushed her spirit long ago, and her stepmother had proven that no one would believe her. If she had once dared to hope that someone would help her, that hope had been stripped away, leaving behind only silence and suffering.

Ella carried the weight of her past alone, sinking further into devastation and depression. No one knew the battles she had fought. No one knew the nightmares that haunted her. And, worst of all, no one ever came to save her.

CHAPTER

5

Free at Last

"Our soul has escaped as a bird from the snare of the fowlers; The snare is broken, and we have escaped."

Psalm 124:7 (NKJV)

I N JANUARY 1990, AFTER months of searching for work without success, Ella finally gathered the courage to ask her father, Henry, if she could move to the United Kingdom. She had rehearsed the conversation in her head, anticipating resistance. And as expected, he was not pleased. He questioned why she wanted to leave, why she couldn't keep trying where she was. But in the end, he had no real reason to deny her. So, with an unenthusiastic nod of approval, Ella had her answer.

On February 22, 1990, she and her younger brother, Noah, boarded a plane with nothing but two small suitcases and £5 each in their pockets. It wasn't much, but they had hope, and that was enough to carry them forward. Upon arrival, they were fortunate to have a cousin already living in the UK, who picked them up from the airport. Noah stayed with him, while Ella was dropped off at their aunt's house—an aunt she barely knew but who had agreed to take her in.

At first, staying with her relatives was a relief. Coming from Nigeria, where family bonds were strong and resources were often shared without question, Ella assumed things would be the same here. But it didn't take long for her to realize that life in the UK operated differently.

Weeks passed, and job applications went unanswered. She lacked the experience most employers were looking for, and with each rejection, she could feel the atmosphere in the house shifting. The warmth and welcome she had initially received were fading.

Her aunt, who had once assured her that she could stay as long as she needed, now seemed impatient. The subtle hints turned into direct comments, and soon, expectations were placed on her. With no income, Ella was forced to apply for jobseeker's allowance. From that, she was required to pay her aunt £30 a week for the use of her front room—an amount that left her with barely anything for herself. There were rules she had to follow, restrictions on visitors, and an ever-present tension that made her feel like an unwanted guest rather than family.

She tried to be understanding. After all, her aunt was helping her in the only way she knew how. But Ella couldn't shake the feeling of discomfort, the sense that she was intruding.

Then, in April 1990, everything changed. She was offered a job as a reservations clerk at the Forum Hotel. The moment she received the news, an overwhelming sense of relief washed over her. At last, she had a foothold, a chance to regain her independence. Without wasting any time, she searched for a place of her own and eventually found a room to rent in a shared house. Her landlord, a kind man named Raj, treated her well, and for the first time in a long while, Ella felt a sense of control over her own life. She stayed in that house for nearly three years, building a routine, finding joy in the simplicity of having a space that was truly hers.

But even as she settled into her new life, something lingered. Ella had left Nigeria hoping to escape, believing that distance could free her from the past. But she soon realized that trauma wasn't something you could outrun. It followed her. It lived in her memories, creeping in when she least expected it. No matter how far she travelled, she carried it with her.

And then there was her father, Henry. He had never been the supportive type. Even during her school and university years, he had never provided what she needed to survive. Now, in a cruel twist, he saw her newfound independence as an opportunity—not for her, but for himself.

He began borrowing money from people back home, assuring them that when they travelled to the UK, Ella would reimburse them. He never discussed this with her, never asked if she was willing or even able to do it. Instead, he simply gave them her phone number and expected her to comply.

The first time she received a call from a stranger claiming her father had promised them money, she was baffled. She assumed it was a mistake. The second time, she confronted him directly. He didn't deny it. Instead, he justified it as "helping with currency exchange," as though it was some harmless transaction. Ella was furious.

"How could you do this without even telling me?" she demanded.

"You're my daughter," he responded, as if that was explanation enough. "You should do as I say."

It was in that moment that Ella saw him for what he truly was — selfish, manipulative, and utterly unconcerned with how his actions affected her. When she told him she couldn't afford to pay, his response was chillingly indifferent.

"Then borrow the money from the bank."

Ella felt something inside her harden. This wasn't love. This wasn't the kind of bond a father and daughter should have. To him, she was nothing more than a means to an end. And for the first time in her life, she fully understood that no matter how far she went, she would never truly be free until she set her own boundaries.

And so with in mind, she made a decision. She would no longer let him control her. She would no longer live in fear of what she had left behind. The past would always be a part of her, but it would not define her.

She had built a life for herself in the UK, one that was hers alone. And that was something no one — not even her father could take away from her.

CHAPTER

A New Start

"Behold, I will do a new thing, Now it shall spring forth; Shall you not know it? I will even make a road in the wilderness And rivers in the desert."

Isaiah 43:19 (NKJV)

THE TAXI RIDE TO the train station was unexpectedly swift, despite the relentless rain drumming against the windows and blurring the cityscape outside. She had anticipated a sluggish journey through waterlogged streets, but to her surprise, traffic was light, and the driver expertly navigated through the downpour without delay. There was hardly any time to exchange pleasantries, let alone engage in a full conversation.

As she arrived at the station, Ella glanced at her watch and exhaled with relief — there was still plenty of time before departure. Unhurried, she made her way to the platform, her excitement mounting. This trip to Belfast had been in the works for weeks, a much-needed weekend escape with friends. They had eagerly planned to visit the Titanic Museum and explore the awe-inspiring Giant's Causeway, immersing themselves in the rich history and natural beauty of Northern Ireland.

Stepping onto the train, she sought out a comfortable window seat, relishing the thought of watching the countryside unfold before her. As the train pulled away from the station, gathering speed, she leaned back, allowing herself a moment to soak in the scenery. Just then, her eyes caught a breathtaking sight—a rainbow arching gracefully across the rain-washed sky, its vivid colours glowing against the retreating storm clouds.

A soft smile played on her lips as she gazed at the natural wonder and the covenant God made with Noah in Genesis chapter 9, where He needed to start the world afresh with Noah and his family after the flood.

There was something poetic about its timing, a silent affirmation of new beginnings. It reminded her of a time, not so long ago, when she had needed a fresh start. The past had been riddled with pain and struggles, but she had found the strength to move forward, to carve out a new path for herself.

Much like the well-known adage, "when it rains, it pours," the blessings that God bestows can often come in abundance. This was certainly true for Ella.

In June 1991, she wholeheartedly committed her life to Christ, and became in new creation in Him. This marked the beginning of a profound journey filled with hope, renewal, and divine purpose.

It was this miraculous encounter that set the stage for the abundant grace and opportunities that would follow.

The second remarkable encounter in Ella's life took place a few years after she had settled in England, when she met Jason. Their paths had crossed on two previous occasions, albeit briefly. The first encounter was in Nigeria, through his brother, Sam, who had been a close friend of Ella's since their sixth form days and throughout university.

The second was when Sam moved to the United Kingdom, he and Ella reconnected, and through him, she met Jason once again. These fleeting interactions set the stage for a deeper connection that would unfold between Ella and Jason. Back then, their meeting had been nothing more than a passing moment, a casual introduction with no real significance. But life has a way of bringing people together at the right time.

As they spent more time together, their bond deepened, and soon, they found themselves in a relationship.

At first, Ella hesitated. Jason was Sam's brother, and she worried that if things didn't work out, it might jeopardize the friendship she cherished so deeply. But despite her fears, their connection only grew stronger. A year after they rekindled their acquaintance, Jason asked her to marry him. It felt like a whirlwind, but it also felt right. In 1993, they stood before family and friends, vowing to love and support each other through life's challenges. Yet, beneath the joy of her new life, Ella carried wounds too deep to ignore.

Trusting Jason had been difficult. She wanted to be fully present in the marriage, to give herself to him completely, but the scars of her past held her back. The memories of abuse, the pain inflicted by someone who should have protected her, haunted her. She tried to keep it buried, to push forward without looking back, but one day, the weight of it all became unbearable. The words escaped her lips before she could stop them.

She told Jason everything. He listened in stunned silence as she revealed the horrors of her past — the beatings, the starvation, the torment, and, worst of all, the abuse at the hands of her own father. When she finally stopped speaking, her breath ragged from the effort of reliving it all, Jason's face was etched with shock and sorrow.

"Your own father?" he whispered, his voice heavy with disbelief.

Ella nodded. She told him she had severed all ties with her father, Henry, that she had no intention of ever speaking to him again. She could never forgive him for what he had done. But Jason, in his quiet and patient way, urged her to reconsider.

"If you don't forgive him, Ella, you'll be the one carrying this pain forever," he told her gently. "Forgiveness isn't for him — it's for you."

His words angered her at first. How could he ask this of her? How could anyone expect her to forgive the man who had stolen her innocence, who had destroyed her sense of safety, who had left her with wounds that still bled? She wrestled with her emotions for days, questioning God, questioning justice, questioning the very idea of forgiveness. But deep down, she knew Jason was right.

One day, with her heart pounding, Ella picked up the phone and dialled her father's number. When he answered, she wasted no time.

"I remember everything," she told him. "I remember what you did. And I forgive you."

There was silence on the other end of the line before he scoffed. "What are you talking about? What did I do?"

Ella felt her hands tremble, but she steadied herself. Calmly, she laid it all out — the abuse, the trauma, the suffering he had caused. She told him she could never forget, but she was choosing to forgive. Still, he denied it.

She hadn't expected an apology, and she didn't get one. But when she hung up, she realized something — she had done what she needed to do. Whether he accepted it or not, she had freed herself from the chains of his control. She refused to let his sins define her any longer.

Yet, forgiving him didn't mean letting him back into her life. For years, Ella kept her distance. Jason occasionally called to check on him, but she never spoke to him directly. She had done her part, and that was enough.

CHAPTER

Betrayal

"Even my own familiar friend in whom I trusted, Who ate my bread, Has lifted up his heel against me.
Psalm 41:9 (NKJV)

YEARS LATER, ELLA found herself longing for a deeper sense of healing. She had spent a lifetime carrying her burdens alone, suffocating under the weight of memories she rarely spoke of. Jason was the only person she had ever confided in, but even with him, there were things she held back — wounds too raw to touch, fears too deep to name.

But silence had not healed her. If anything, it had kept her trapped, reliving the past in the shadows of her own mind. She knew she couldn't continue like this. She needed guidance, wisdom — someone who could help her navigate the tangled pain she had buried for so long.

During a church retreat, she found herself drawn to the pastor's wife, a woman known for her kindness and gentle spirit. There was something reassuring about her presence, the way she listened without judgment, her voice soft and understanding. For the first time in years, Ella felt safe enough to speak. She poured out her heart, unravelling the painful memories she had kept locked away. She spoke of the loneliness, the betrayals, the years of feeling like she didn't belong. She spoke of the abuse — the way it had stolen her childhood and left her with wounds that never quite closed.

The woman listened intently; her eyes filled with empathy. She offered words of comfort, promising to pray for Ella's healing, reminding her that God saw her pain and had not abandoned her. For the first time in a long time, Ella allowed herself to believe in hope. She left the retreat feeling lighter, as if, for the first time, someone was truly walking alongside her in her healing journey. But the feeling didn't last.

That Sunday, as she sat in the pews, listening to the pastor's sermon, a strange unease settled over her. He was speaking on fatherhood — about different kinds of fathers, the role they played in shaping their children's lives. At first, it seemed like any other sermon. But then, his tone shifted.

"There are fathers," he said, his voice growing heavier, "who fail in their responsibilities. Fathers who neglect their children. Fathers who abandon them." He paused, scanning the congregation. "And then," he continued, his voice laced with disgust, "there are those who abuse their children—sick, twisted individuals who rob the innocent of their dignity and leave scars that never truly heal."

Ella's breath caught in her throat. A cold, sinking feeling gripped her chest. No one else knew.
She had only told Jason. And the pastor's wife.
Her heart pounded as realization hit her. The pastor wasn't just speaking in general terms. He knew! And he was talking about her.

Her hands trembled as she gripped the armrest of her seat, trying to steady herself. The walls of the church suddenly felt too close; the air too thick. She wanted to disappear, to sink into the floor, to run. She forced herself to keep breathing, but her mind was racing. Who else knows? Who else did they tell?

Had that been the only issue, it might have been bearable. His gaze was fixed directly on her, singling her out without saying her name. Then, without warning, he took it a step further and asked if anyone present had gone through such an experience to stand up so that he could pray for them.

A cold wave of panic washed over Ella. Her body refused to move. She just sat there, frozen in place, with her heart pounding profusely in her chest.

Every second felt like an eternity. She barely remembered the rest of the sermon. The words blurred together, drowned out by the sound of her own pulse roaring in her ears.

That night, she confronted Jason. He tried to reassure her, suggesting that maybe the pastor's wife had shared the burden with her husband. Ella felt her stomach twist. "Then why didn't she tell me? Why didn't she warn me?" Her voice cracked. "I trusted her. I trusted her."

"She used my pain as conversation material." Ella said, her voice barely above a whisper. "And he turned it into a sermon."

The betrayal hit her like a fresh wound. She had spent years keeping her past locked away, carefully choosing who to trust, and now — now it had been laid bare, twisted into a lesson for strangers to hear. She felt exposed, humiliated.

"I can't go back there," she said finally, her voice hollow. Jason didn't argue. He kept going to church without her at first, but it wasn't the same. The trust had been broken. The place that was supposed to be a sanctuary had become another reminder of betrayal. Over time, Jason, too, began to see it. The weight of what had happened pressed between them, unspoken but undeniable. Eventually, they both left the church.

They needed a fresh start. A place where Ella's pain wouldn't be turned into a sermon. A place where healing didn't come with conditions. A place where she could finally be free.

CHAPTER

8

Healed and Restored

"He heals the brokenhearted And binds up their wounds."

Psalm 147:3 (NKJV)

AFTER A FEW MONTHS of searching, Jason and Ella found a new church — one that felt different from the rest. There were no prying eyes, no whispered betrayals. It was a place where people truly listened, where healing was encouraged, not exploited. For the first time in a long time, Ella felt safe.

This church became a sanctuary for their family, a haven where she could finally breathe without fear of judgment. She no longer felt like a story to be told behind closed doors, but a person — worthy of love, of understanding, of restoration.

At first, she kept her guard up. She had learned the hard way that trust was not something to be given freely. But as the weeks turned into months, she found herself surrounded by people who genuinely cared, who saw her not as a victim but as someone capable of healing and growth.

Counselling became a turning point. For years, she had carried the weight of shame, believing — somewhere deep inside — that maybe, just maybe, she had done something to deserve what had happened to her. But through therapy, through prayer, through the steady support of those who truly wished to see her whole, she began to accept a truth that had eluded her for so long: None of it was her fault.

With that realization came another fear — one that had haunted her ever since she and Jason talked about having children. She had spent her life trapped in a cycle of pain, being passed from one cruel hand to another. What if she wasn't strong enough to break it? What if her trauma, the darkness of her past, somehow seeped into her own parenting?

She refused to let that happen. Ella made a vow: her children would never experience what she had endured. They would know love, safety, and security. They would never go to sleep questioning whether they were loved or wanted. They would never feel invisible.

In 1993, her first child, Peter, was born. Holding him in her arms for the first time, she felt something shift deep inside her—a fierce, unshakable resolve. Every whispered doubt, every fear that she wouldn't be enough, disappeared the moment she looked into his eyes. She would protect him. No matter what.

Four years later, in 1997, they welcomed another son, and in 2003, their daughter completed their family.

Ella cherished them fiercely, watching over them with an attentiveness that some might have called overprotective. She was mindful of who they spent time with, careful about where they went. She never wanted to be the kind of mother who suffocated her children with fear, but she also knew what could happen when no one was watching.

"If anyone ever makes you feel uncomfortable, you come to me," she told them often. "No matter who it is. No matter what they say."

She drilled it into them, over and over again, because she knew how easily a child's trust could be manipulated, how predators thrived in silence. As her children grew into adulthood, she never stopped reminding them to stay aware. Some people called her overzealous, overly cautious. But she had seen too much, endured too much, to take chances. She had once been a little girl who had no one to protect her, and she would never let her children feel that same fear.

But despite her vigilance, she did not raise them in fear. She raised them in love. She made sure they knew laughter and warmth, that their home was a place of joy, not just caution. She taught them that while the world could be cruel, it was also full of kindness, of good people, of second chances.

Ella had walked through the fire. She had been burned, scarred, nearly destroyed. But she had not been consumed. And for that, she is grateful.

"We are hard-pressed on every side, yet not crushed; we are perplexed, but not in despair; 9 persecuted, but not forsaken; struck down, but not destroyed." 2 Corinthians 4:8-12 (NKJV)

CHAPTER

9

Finding Purpose

"Blessed be the God and Father of our Lord Jesus Christ, the Father of mercies and God of all comfort, 4 who comforts us in all our tribulation, that we may be able to comfort those who are in any trouble, with the comfort with which we ourselves are comforted by God."

2 Corinthians 1:3-4 (NKJV)

WHO COULD HAVE imagined that Ella, someone who had endured such unimaginable abuse and neglect, would one day create a loving, peaceful home? If the world had its way, she might have never had a chance to rise above her painful past, for it would have been so easy for her to be swallowed up by the darkness that once threatened to define her. But in a way that only the divine could orchestrate, God, in His boundless mercy, whispered His grace into her heart and poured out His unfathomable love upon her.

Through His infinite grace, Ella's life took a turn that no one, not even she, could have foreseen. God, in His perfect timing and wisdom, wove every painful thread of her life into a tapestry of redemption.

Where once there was only despair, He has brought forth hope. Where there was once brokenness, He has brought restoration.

The Bible says, *"And we know that all things work together for good to those who love God, to those who are the called according to His purpose"* Romans 8:28 (NKJV).

This truth has never been more evident than in Ella's life. What the enemy intended for evil, God has used for good. Just like Joseph's experience in Genesis 50:20.

Every tear that Ella shed, every painful step she took, God has turned into a stepping stone toward her healing and transformation. No longer is she a victim of her circumstances, but a living testament to God's ability to heal and restore even the deepest wounds.

Today, she has become a beacon of hope, a vessel in the hands of the Almighty, used to impact the lives of others in ways she could never have imagined.

Through her journey, Ella has become a vessel God is using to champion change, pouring into the lives of parents and children who have faced similar struggles. She speaks into the hearts of the broken, offering them the same hope and healing that she herself received. Her story is not just one of survival, but of triumph. She has walked through fire, and now, with every word she speaks and every life she touches, she leads others into the light of restoration.

God has taken her scars and turned them into a source of strength, using her experiences to help others find the courage to heal and the strength to rebuild their lives.

Her impact is far-reaching, bringing families to a place where they can experience true healing, hope, and restoration. What seemed impossible for Ella is now a beautiful reality—a life transformed by God's grace, and a legacy of love and resilience passed on to future generations.

To every survivor who has ever felt unseen, unheard, or broken—you are not alone. This book is a testament that healing is possible, and hope is real. And to those who have walked through the fire and wondered if they would ever feel whole again—this is for you. You are stronger than you know, and healing is within reach with the help of God, Jehovah Rapha, our Healer.

www.ingramcontent.com/pod-product-compliance
Lightning Source LLC
Chambersburg PA
CBHW071822020426
42331CB00007B/1588

* 9 7 8 1 9 1 1 3 1 2 3 7 6 *